LOVE YOURSELF
enough to take the
actions required for
your happiness...

LOVE YOURSELF
enough to cut
yourself loose
from the ties of
the drama-filled
past...

LOVE YOURSELF
enough to move on!

Dr. Steve Maraboli

This journal belongs to:

_____

MISGUIDED

mis·guid·ed

Websters Definition:
led or prompted by wrong or
inappropriate motives or
ideals

Many of us have been misguided and experienced challenges that have impacted our perception of self. Extreme self-hate, low self-esteem, no self-worth....these realities make it impossible to live life to the fullest. The goal of this journal is to promote healing and build self-love in all areas of your life. Through interactive activities and reflective prompts, you will become aware of your needs and discover how to accept and love your true self.

What if you simply devoted this year to love yourself more?

Getting to know
YOU

Part of self-love is getting to know who you are apart from your roles in life (child, parent, friend, student, etc.). Who are YOU?

Greatest Fear:

Greatest accomplishment:

What I love about my life:

What I don't like about my life:

What I love about myself:

What I dislike about myself:

What I need to work on:

My biggest regret:

My dreams and/or goals for the next 6 months:

What do you
SEE?

Self-portraits may be created impromptu
from memory or from mirrors.

Using the diagram, create (draw, color, etc.)
an image of yourself based on how you think
people see you vs. how you see yourself.

For example: others see me as strong, happy,
long hair, made up and I see myself as
someone who wears wigs and make up,
depressed, self-conscious etc.

How I think other people see me:

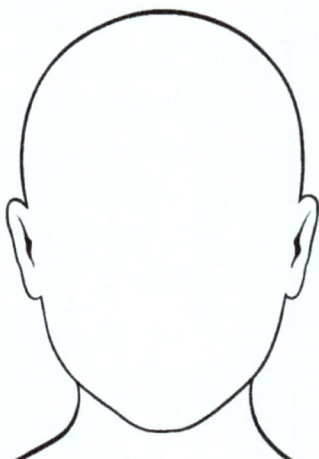

How I see myself:

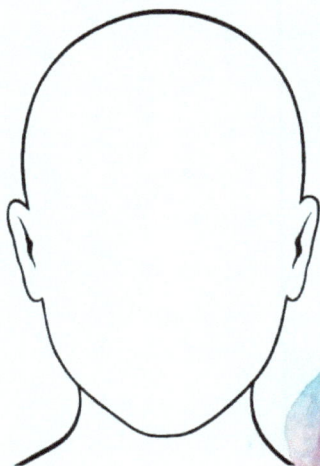

NOTES | THOUGHTS | REFLECTIONS

Do you love YOUReSELF?

☐ YES ☐ NO

Explain why you feel that way:

What is self-love to
YOU?

Which of these matches your definition of self-love? Feel free to choose more than 1 or add an item to the list.

[ ] Thinking about yourself, your wants, your needs, and then acting on those things

[ ] Putting in the effort to create a life that you truly love instead of settling for unhappiness

[ ] Engaging in relationships that lift you up and make you feel fulfilled

[ ] Taking care of your mental and physical health.... equally Not being so hard on yourself all the time

[ ] Giving yourself the grace to make mistakes and learn from them

[ ] Forgiving yourself for things you did and mistakes you made days, weeks, months, or years ago

[ ] Nurturing your growth by learning new things and trying new experiences

[ ] Spending time doing things you love and not putting others desires first

[ ] Managing your daily stress and not just pushing through it

[ ] Embracing your authentic self: the good, the bad, the ugly

[ ] Re-directing self-destructive thoughts and behaviors to healthier coping skills

[ ] Unconditional Love

self-love is
NOT

Which of these do you struggle with?
Feel free to choose more than 1 or add an item to
the list.

- [ ] Putting others before yourself which in turn hurts you emotionally, physically, and mentally

- [ ] Telling yourself that you will love yourself when: you lose weight, accomplish goals, finish school, get married, etc.

- [ ] Accepting behavior that makes you uncomfortable or feel violated and not saying anything about it

- [ ] Putting yourself in dangerous or unhealthy situations

- [ ] Ignoring the problems in your life

- [ ] Having no interests, hobbies, goals, or life outside of the other people in your life

- [ ] Negative self-talk

- [ ] Masking your true feelings

- [ ] Uncontrollable anger

Things I love about
MYSELF

List 5 things you love about yourself:

1.

2.

3.

4.

5.

It's time to
HEAL!

In order to love yourself, you have to be an
advocate for your own healing and recovery!
This means doing the work yourself
or doing the work with someone else like a
therapist, peer coach, support
group, friend, doctor, etc.

Healing happens when YOU start the process.
To start the healing process, you must first
admit that you've been hurt.

Once you admit that you have been hurt, you
have to acknowledge who and what caused the
hurt.

This section allows you to acknowledge,
analyze, process, and overcome the emotional
damage that the hurt caused.

What things are hurting you right now?

What's the most painful thing you've experienced?
How does it affect you emotionally, mentally, and
physically? How has it changed you?

What steps can you take towards healing?

What regrets do you have in your life as a result of this pain?

What mistakes have you made that you haven't forgiven yourself for?

Have you used the hurt/pain to sabotage your life/job/relationships? Why?

Have you used the hurt/pain to sabotage your life/job/relationships? Why?

Do you need closure from any events or relationships in your life? Write about those feelings.

Self-care is the
BEST CARE!

Once you heal in some areas of your life you begin to realize that it is perfectly ok to take care of yourself.

What good are you to others if you are not good to yourself?

Self-love = the act of loving who you are.
Self-care = actions you perform to take care of your physical, emotional, spiritual, and mental needs.

There are several components to self-care:

PHYSICAL   EMOTIONAL   PERSONAL   SOCIAL

PROFESSIONAL   ENVIRONMETAL   FINANCIAL

Self-care

PHYSICAL

Physical self-care means taking care of your physical needs such as getting proper amounts of water, food, sleep, and physical activity.

WHAT AREAS OF PHYSICAL SELF-CARE ARE YOU GREAT AT?

o Healthy Eating   o Pampering Your Body o Taking Breaks
o Physical Activity o Going to the Doctor
o Getting Sleep   o Body Image

WHAT AREAS OF PHYSICAL SELF-CARE NEED THE MOST IMPROVEMENT?

o Healthy Eating   o Pampering Your Body o Taking Breaks
o Physical Activity o Going to the Doctor
o Getting Sleep   o Body Image

WHAT STEPS CAN YOU TAKE TO IMPROVE THOSE AREAS OF YOUR LIFE?

Self-care

EMOTIONAL

Dealing with your emotions in a healthy way. Instead
of acting out, shutting down, or being destructive...choose healthy
alternatives to positively deconstruct strong emotions.

WHAT AREAS OF EMOTIONAL SELF-CARE ARE YOU GREAT AT?

o Coping Skills
o Expressing
  Feelings
o Recognizing
  Feelings

o Self-Talk
o Compassion
o Releasing Feelings

o Processing
  Feelings
o Self-Soothing
o Mental Health

WHAT AREAS OF EMOTIONAL SELF-CARE NEED THE MOST IMPROVEMENT?

o Coping Skills
o Expressing
  Feelings
o Recognizing
  Feelings

o Self-Talk
o Compassion
o Releasing Feelings

o Processing
  Feelings
o Self-Soothing
o Mental Health

WHAT STEPS CAN YOU TAKE TO IMPROVE THOSE AREAS OF YOUR LIFE?

PERSONAL

Learning about YOU! Who you are, what you like,
what you enjoy doing. Having goals and interests that are just for
you.

WHAT AREAS OF PERSONAL SELF-CARE ARE YOU GREAT AT?

- o Knowing Yourself
- o Firm Beliefs
- o Not Needing Approval
- o Time for Hobbies
- o Working Toward Goals
- o Alone Time
- o Standing Up for Yourself

WHAT AREAS OF PERSONAL SELF-CARE NEED THE MOST IMPROVEMENT?

- o Knowing Yourself
- o Firm Beliefs
- o Not Needing Approval
- o Time for Hobbies
- o Working Toward Goals
- o Alone Time
- o Standing Up for Yourself

WHAT STEPS CAN YOU TAKE TO IMPROVE THOSE AREAS OF YOUR LIFE?

Self-care

SOCIAL

Understanding your social needs and creating boundaries that respect them.

WHAT AREAS OF SOCIAL SELF-CARE ARE YOU GREAT AT?

o Reaching Out   o Solid Friendships   o Balancing Life
o Communicating   o Setting Boundaries   + Friends
o Quality Time

WHAT AREAS OF SOCIAL SELF-CARE NEED THE MOST IMPROVEMENT?

o Saying No   o Quality Time
o Communicating   o Setting Boundaries   o Repairing Your
o Reaching Out   o Give & Take   Friendships

WHAT STEPS CAN YOU TAKE TO IMPROVE THOSE AREAS OF YOUR LIFE?

Self-care
PRACTICAL

Self-care also includes taking care of your practical day to day needs, honoring your needs in every situation.

PROFESSIONAL SELF-CARE

Continuing to learn and advance in your field. Having a job that makes you happy. Having a proper work/life balance.

ENVIRONMENTAL SELF-CARE

Toxic environments are slow killers. Making sure that you're in a healthy environment is key.

FINANCIAL SELF-CARE

Budgeting, paying bills on time, saving money all contribute to healthy living.

CONSIDER THE FOLLOWING:

Are you happy with your job?

What needs aren't being met?

How are your finances?

Are you happy with your savings/spending?

Is your work/church/spiritual environment safe or is it toxic?

What steps can you take to improve these areas of your life?

Time to
BRAIN DUMP

A brain dump is pretty much exactly what it sounds like. It's taking pen to paper and getting all your thoughts OUT of your brain. It is a way to release stumbling thoughts and face each thought individually instead of compounding them over time.

Dealing with yourself, your wants, desires, hurts, and other feelings that arise, brain dumping can be a helpful tool in managing your emotional needs as well as your practical needs.

- Grab a pen and notepad or use this one :)
- Create a list using the below headings
- HONESTLY evaluate your list
- Complete your list (date-mark when you complete items on your list)

MUST	WANT	PERHAPS
Things you've committed to doing Example: Pay the mortgage	Things you would like to do but haven't committed to them yet Example: Call my friends	Things you may want to do at some point but are far down on the priority list Example: Travel to Dubai

MUST	WANT	PERHAPS

What is my
VALUE?

Self-acceptance is a specific stage in self-discovery that occurs whenever a person is willing to look at themselves objectively. When they do, they will realize that their strengths far outweigh their weaknesses.

REFLECTIONS

Reflect on these questions and try to answer them honestly.

This exercise can give you the opportunity to validate your positive self-perception:

1. What 3 things do I like about myself?

2. What are my strengths?

3. What activities can make me a better and stronger person?

MY VOWS

What promises or commitments are you ready to make
to yourself right now? Write them here.
Add a completion date on the ones that you have completed:

I PROMISE/COMMIT TO...

www.ingramcontent.com/pod-product-compliance
Lightning Source LLC
Chambersburg PA
CBHW041811040426
42449CB00004B/150